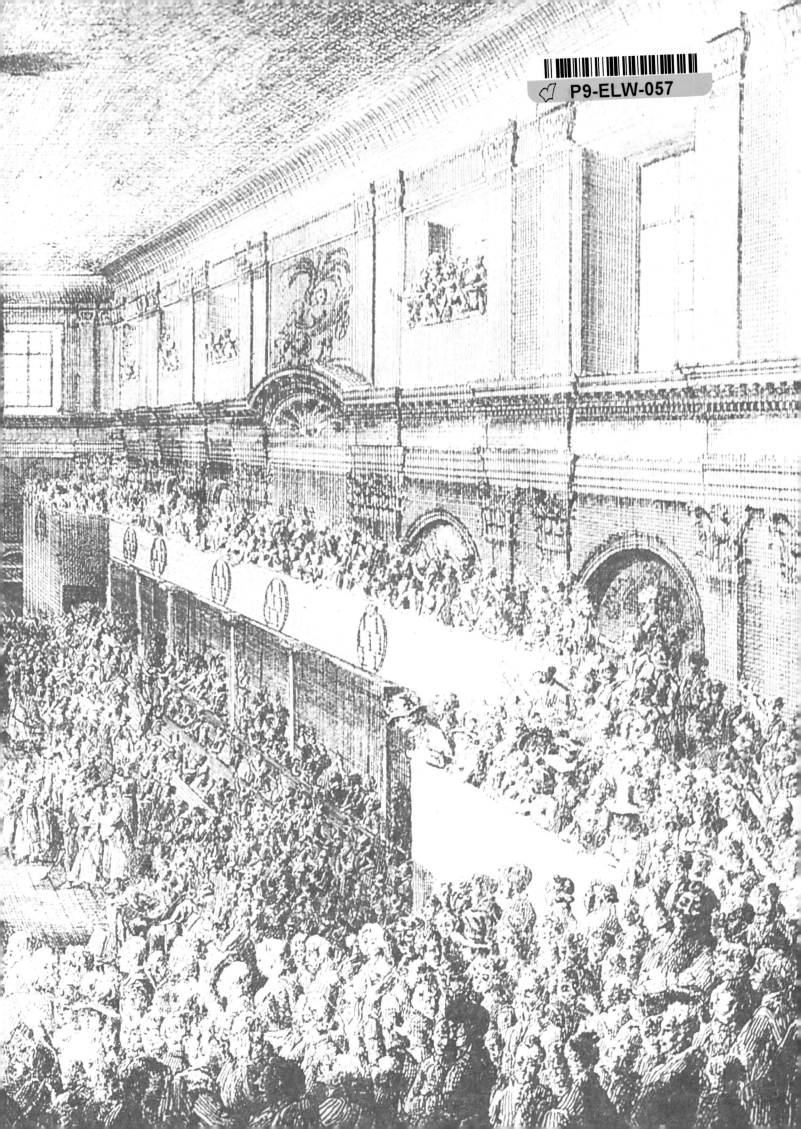

POLAND

PHOTOGTRAPHS
STANISŁAWA, KRZYSZTOF AND RAFAŁ JABŁOŃSKI

TEXT
WOJCIECH FIJAŁKOWSKI

WARSAW 1999

TRANSLATION
Robert Strybel

Photographs from the St. K. and R. Jabłońskis Photolibrary, tel; (22) 42-27-72, (22) 642-06-71

Print: Perfekt, Warszawa ul. Połczyńska 99, tel 36 52 78

ISBN 83-900690-7-5

POLAND

Poland, a country situated in the very heart of Europe, today occupies an area similar to the historical frontiers of the Polish state that emerged towards the end of the 10th century.

The stages of the development of Poland's territory over the centuries were similar to that of other European nations. In about the year 1500 BC, Pre-Slavonic and Slavonic peoples began settling what would become Poland. This process lasted nearly 1,000 years.

Among the many different tribes inhabiting the lands between the Rivers Odra and Bug and between the Baltic and the Carpathians, the most dynamic were the Polanians and Vistulians. The Polanians lived in the basin of the middle and lower Warta (in the west of the country), and the richest of the tribes, the numerous Vistulians, dwelt along the upper Vistula. Home was usually a wooden settlement comprising several homesteads which were grouped round an open square or irregular road in order to facilitate the common use of natural resources.

The people, who settled there two centuries before the rise of the Polish state, organised themselves into small territorial communities. For protection they were surrounded by moats and palisades or earth-and-timber ramparts with an entrance gate as at the well-known Biskupin settlement from the Lusatian period.

The chief centre of the Polanians was Gniezno. There, on a towering hill surrounded by forests and water, a fortified town was built. It consisted of the town proper, two fortified boroughs inhabited by craftsmen and an open settlement on the outskirts with a separate marketplace. In time, the latter evolved into the town's commercial and residential centre.

Under the rule of the native Piast dynasty, from at least the mid-9th century the Polanians began to expand territorially, extending their authority to other Slavonic tribes. By the end of the 10th century, the Vistulians, whose main centre was in Kraków, also came under the sway of the Polanians. Thus was formed the nucleus of the future all-Polish state which would take its name from the Polanians.

Its creator and first historical ruler was Mieszko I. By accepting Christianity in 966 he completed a many-year-long period of internal consolidation. He welded together a structure of authority and strengthened the territorial foundations of the young state. Poland thus entered the political system of Central European countries and embarked on a Christian road of development, which afforded her wide access to the civilisation and cultural advancements of Western Europe.

As Poland's Christianisation progressed, amid the wooden buildings of the fortified towns there began appearing the first stone religious structures in the form of rotunda-like chapels. Such places of worship could be found on Wawel hill in Kraków, in Gniezno and neighbouring Ostrów Lednicki as well as in Wiślica, Giecz and Przemyśl.

A bit later the building of small, single-nave parish churches with towers over their main entrances began. Like the chapels, they were built of granite blocks.

The first stage of Poland's Christianisation was concluded during the reign of Bolesław the Brave, Mieszko's son. The crowning touch of that process was an historic convention in Gniezno in the year 1000, personally attended by German Emperor Otto III. The convention not only attested to Poland's strong position in Central Europe but also sanctioned an independent Polish ecclesiastical structure with bishoprics in Poznań, Kraków, Wrocław and Kołobrzeg and its metropolitan see in Gniezno. The construction of cathedral churches, three-naved stone basilicas with twin-towered façades, got under way in those towns the moment the bishoprics were established.

The Gniezno of the first Piasts was not only the chief ecclesiastical see but also the capital of the state. There, in 1025, Bolesław the Brave was crowned king of Poland. Continuing the work of his father, he enhanced the power of the early-feudal Polish state. He also took up the idea of Mieszko I to expand his political influence to neighbouring Slavonic lands.

After Poznań and Gniezno had been largely destroyed by foreign invaders and internal strife in Poland, the grandson of Bolesław the Brave, Kazimierz the Restorer, in about 1038 moved the capital to Kraków. During his reign and that of his successors, for much of the Middle Ages, Kraków was truly the centre of Poland's political and administrative life. It was the seat of Polish kings and princes as well as being an important cultural and religious centre with numerous churches, monasteries and a cathedral school.

From the 11th to the 14th centuries, a great variety of religious structures were erected in Kraków, ranging from small stone churches to gothic brick-and-stone basilicas. Of the greatest significance for the new Polish capital was the construction site atop Wawel Hill, where a fortified royal castle complex was built from the 11th to 13th centuries. There, the son of Kazimierz the Restorer, Władysław Herman, erected a second Romanesque Wawel cathedral named after St Wenceslaus. It included the big Crypt of St Leonard, which for centuries would serve as the place of interment of Poland's monarchs.

Congregations of monks coming to Poland as missionaries paved the way for the development of sacred mediaeval architecture in Kraków and its environs as well as in other parts of the country. The first were the Benedictines arriving from Italy and the Franco-Belgian borderlands. They erected magnificent churches and monasteries preferably at inaccessible, out-of-the-way building sites, where self-contained monastic complexes could isolate them from the outside world. The biggest abbey of the Rhineland Benedictines was founded in 1044 at Tyniec on the Vistula near Kraków by Kazimierz the Restorer, who had been educated by the Benedictines.

The Cistercians, a reformed branch of the Benedictines enjoying the protection of princes and bishops, arrived in Wrocław, founded the Church of St Vincent in Wrocław.

The Dominicans and Franciscans, both mendicant (begging) orders, were concerned mainly with pastoral and charitable activity among the masses. Their monasteries and churches were therefore located in densely populated urban areas.

A great role in the spread of mediaeval religious architecture was also played by clerical founders and representatives of wealthy Polish clans. Among the clergy, well-known patrons in the 12th century were the brothers Alexander and Walter from Malonne, Belgium, installed in the bishoprics of Płock and Wrocław by the Archbishop of Gniezno, Jakub of Żnin. Through their efforts, magnificent Romanesque cathedrals displaying traces of Franco-Flemish influence were erected in both those towns.

Exceptional patrons of the Church in the early Middle Ages were members of the knightly Łabędź clan who founded more than a dozen churches. Most of them were

Panorama of the Warsaw "Baryczkowska", 1755-1779.

Poland in the late 12th century. The Benedictines' most magnificent monastic complexes, whose architectural centrepiece was always a church, were built in Sulejów, Jędrzejów, Wąchock and Mogiła, leaving a permanent imprint on the cultural landscape of the Kraków, Kielce and Piotrków regions respectively. Impressive church and monastery complexes, which have survived down to the present, were also erected in Kołbacz and Oliwa and subsequently at Pelpin.

At almost the same time as the Cistercians, the Dominicans began arriving. They were brought to Poland from Bologna by Blessed Jacek Odrowąż, who first installed them in Kraków in 1221 and five years later - in Sandomierz. It was there they built their first monastery including a Romanesque-Gothic Church of St James.

Somewhat later than the Dominicans, the Bohemian Brothers Minor, known as Franciscans, set foot on Polish territory. It was for them that Henryk the Bearded of the Silesian Piast line founded the monastery and church of St Francis in Kraków. His son, Prince Henryk the Pious of

attributed to the clan's most outstanding representative, Piotr Włostkowic, who provided the funds for the big Benedictine monastery at Ołbin and the monastery and church of the Blessed Virgin Mary in the Wrocław district of Piasek. Another aristocrat, the voivod Sieciech, founded the twin-towered Church of St Andrew in Kraków. The castellan of Kujawy, Piotr Wszczeborowic, provided the resources needed to build the Norbertine Cloister and Church of St Prokop in Strzelno near Gniezno.

Like many other mediaeval European states, Poland from the 10th to 12th centuries was a monarchy, whose rulers considered it their dynastic property and legacy. But the progressing feudalisation of social relations gradually led to the disintegration of the dynastic rulers' strong centralised authority. This eventually brought about the break-up of the state into separate regions. A thus fragmented Poland became easy prey to destructive invasions by Prussians, Tartars and Mongols. To safeguard the lands of northern Poland against Prussian invasions, Prince Konrad of Masovia brought the Knights of the Order of the

6

Blessed Virgin Mary to the Chełmno region. After establishing themselves, the Teutonic Knights or the Knights of the Cross (as the German order was known), turned their might against Poland.

Fortunately, the break-up of Polish lands did not destroy the elements uniting the nation and the sense of belonging to the Regnum Poloniae on the part of the independent Piast princes. All the regions began to develop economically, trade was stepped up and the use of money became widespread. Great landed estates began appearing and colonists, mainly of German nationality, began settling rural areas. The urban population also grew as new towns were established or rebuilt on the basis of the German-style Magdeburg Charter or its Polish version, the Chełmno Charter. In addition to Polish and German inhabitants in these towns, there was a growing percentage of Jews who in 1264 had received a special set of privileges from Bolesław the Pious.

In the late 13th century, several regional princes undertook steps to reunify the state, but that was not achieved until the early 14th century by King Władysław the Short. It has his son. Kazimierz the Great, who continued that task and created a flourishing country. The Poland of Kazimierz the Great was a well-organised state. Surrounded by an entourage of trusted ministers, the king carried out a consistent programme to internally unite the country, unify its monetary and tax system and stabilise Poland's position in the European arena.

All this helped to transform the country economically and socially, activated the economy and increased the prosperity of all social classes. There was also quite a bit of building going on in town and countryside alike. It was said of Kazimierz the Great that "he had found a Poland built of wood but left behind one built of brick and stone." Indeed, the king himself was the main motor force behind every manner of building project, and his good husbandry coupled with his broad cultural, scholarly and educational aspirations, were worthy of the greatest European monarchs. Through his efforts, more than 100 religious and secular edifices of various kinds were erected. Of particular note were castles and town fortifications forming a part of the country's defence system planned by the king. In creating this new system, the king benefited from the military-construction experience of the Teutonic Knights, whose most splendid fortified structure was the gothic monastery and castle complex, built in stages in the 14th and 15th centuries in Malbork.

Of great importance to the development of Poland's culture and learning was the university founded by Kazimierz the Great in 1364, then known as the Kraków Academy. From 1491 to 1495 among its students was the great astronomer Mikołaj Kopernik (Copernicus).

Also during the reign of Kazimierz the Great, the development of Gothic architecture reached its apogee. During the 14th century, old Romanesque cathedrals were transformed to reflect the new style. Numerous churches being built or rebuilt at that time in nearly every part of the country were given soaring Gothic spires.

The picture of the religious edifices dominating the landscape of mediaeval Poland would be incomplete if one failed to mention the sculptures associated with Romanesque and Gothic church architecture.

Romanesque sculpture, which was mainly an architectural sculpture, enlivened the surface of church walls, filled the portals of main and side church entrances and adorned both columns and their capitals.

A magnificent work of Romanesque art were the bronze doors of Gniezno Cathedral portraying the life, mission and martyr's death in Prussia of St. Adalbert.

The stone sculpture of the Gothic period, continuing in its early period the tradition of stone architectural sculpture, now began expressing itself in new forms. One example were the monumental royal tombs inside Wawel Cathedral. A high level of artistry was displayed by the sculpted tomb of Władysław the Short, created in the 14th century, as well as by the canopied mausoleum of Kazimierz the Great.

An important artistic element adorning churches and promoting religious formation were murals, which have largely not survived down to the present, and stained-glass gracing pointed-arch windows and the circular rosettes found at the top of portals.

Although Poland was said to have turned from wood to stone during the reign of the last Piast monarch, in actuality wooden architecture remained quite widespread. That material was used to build both churches and secular structures. That included manor-houses big and small - the seats of the Polish nobility whose role in the country's social and political life was growing.

After Kazimierz the Great had died without leaving an heir, on the basis of dynastic agreements the throne went to his nephew, Louis of Hungary. He was succeeded by his daughter Jadwiga. After her marriage to Lithuanian Duke Władysław Jagiełło, she helped to Christianise Lithuania. That opened the way for a political union between Poland and Lithuania, crowned by a treaty of unification signed in Lublin in 1569.

A quarter of a century after Władysław Jagiełło ascended the throne, combined Polish, Lithuanian and Ruthenian forces fought the historic Battle of Grunwald in 1410 against the armies of the Teutonic Knights. The latter suffered a crushing defeat and that enabled Poland to regain the territories she had lost in the north. It also meant that Poland had gained the status of a European power.

In this new political situation, new forms of the country's internal structures began to emerge. A the king's side there emerged a Royal Council which played the role of a senate. Assemblies of the nobility gradually involved into the Sejm (lower house of parliament). By the end of the 15th century, a bicameral parliament had been created in Poland, sanctioned by the parliamentary law enacted in Piotrków Trybunalski in 1493. At the same time, town government developed and exerted growing influence on the expansion of the burgher class.

The economic growth of towns in the 15th century provided new impetus for religious and secular building. That, involved not only architecture but extended to the fine arts and artistic crafts, music, literature and theatre. As a result, they greatly contributed to the development of Polish culture, both in the capital and throughout the country.

The architectural and artistic projects of the House of Vasa in Warsaw, as previously, were emulated by the nobles and aristocrats who built impressive manorhouses and palatial residences surrounded by gardens in the suburbs of Warsaw's Old Town.

But unlike Warsaw, one of Poland's most dynamic buildings sites and artistic centres, other towns regressed considerably as a result of extensive war damage in the first half of the 17th century and because of the anti-burgher policy of the gentry.

The impoverishment of the burghers and stagnation in the building sector contrasted greatly in the first half of the 17th century with the growing prosperity of the gentry and aristocracy, attested to by the splendid residences and churches they were erecting.

The most magnificent, gigantic and downright extravagant aristocratic castle-like residence was Krzyżtopór. It was designed by Wawrzyniec Senes in the mid-17th century at Ujazd near Opatów for the voivod of Sandomierz, Krzysztof Ossoliński.

Church dignitaries, notably the archbishops of Gniezno and the bishop of Kraków, did not allow themselves to be outdone.

One of the most splendid residences and among the best-maintained down to the present was built in Kielce from 1636 to 1646 for the Bishop of Kraków Jakub Zadzik. The Vasa court architect Jan Chrzciciel Trevano designed the palace and it was erected by Tomasz Poncino.

The reign of the Vasas brought a considerable change in the ideology and culture that had prevailed in Poland until then. The secularism of the Renaissance and the liberal humanism of the 16th century began to give way to the powerful offensive of the Counterreformation which gained impetus following the Council of Trent. Being a devout Catholic and staunch advocate of the Catholic Church's ultimate triumph, it is no wonder he was depicted on his memorial column in Warsaw with a cross in one hand and a Polish sword in the other. In his religious involvement, he found support in the main Counterreformation force, the Jesuits. As a dynamic and well-organised order, the Jesuit Fathers soon introduced to all the countries of Europe, including Poland, a Jesuit-style Baroque church of Jesus (Il Gesu) shaped in Rome. The major religious structure funded by Zygmunt III was just such an edifice. That was the Church of Saints Peter and Paul in Kraków, built in the early 17th century by Jan Trevano. Besides that type of church, throughout Poland many magnificent churches not patterned on the Jesuit model were erected through the efforts of Poland's aristocracy.

Since the 15th century, one of the country's most important religious shrines had been Jasna Góra (Bright Mountain) outside Częstochowa. During the reign of the Vasa Dynasty and as a result of their patronage, the Pauline monastic complex was considerably expanded, fortified and turned into a modern four-bastion stronghold. Thanks to that important undertaking, Jasna Góra was able to resists the Swedish invasion of the mid-7th century, and the defence of the shrine became the turning-point in the several-year-old war with Sweden.

Parallel to the erection of magnificent Baroque church buildings, reflecting Europe's prevailing artistic currents of that period, the Counterreformation also brought with it numerous more modest churches still retaining a Gothic-Renaissance design. Erected in the first half of the 17th century mainly by local stonemasons, they were generally endowed with a late-Gothic hull and façade compositions adorned with Renaissance or even manneristic decorations. As such, they blended nicely with the Vistula landscape of Kazimierz Dolny as well as the town architecture of Lublin, Kalisz and Warsaw.

The culture and tastes of the average nobleman of that period were reflected by his single-floor wooden manorhouse with a tall sloped roof and corner alcoves or turrets.

The ideology of Sarmatianism, which had prevailed among the gentry since the late 16th century, gave rise to a typically Polish portrait known as the Sarmatian portrait.

Menor House in Czarnożyły

Its principal trait was a certain severity, perhaps even a brutal, drastically realistic manner of portrayal. Portraits accompanied the nobleman throughout most of his lifetime — in all ceremonies and situations. The coffin portrait, attached to the head of the coffin, was a prominent feature of the pompous and downright theatrical funeral ceremonies then in vogue. Later it was enshrined on the wall of a church or chapel in an ornately-carved frame.

The second half of the 17th century for Poland was a period of trying and tragic ordeals. It was a time of Cossack rebellions and invasions by Swedish and Turkish armies which had a devastating effect on the country's economy, culture and population.

After the Swedish invaders and Cossack rebels had been repulsed and the Turkish armies had been routed at Chocim in 1673, the main hero of that victory, Grand Crown Hetman Jan Sobieski, was elevated to the Polish throne. It was under his reign, encompassing the last quarter of the 17th century, that a national reconstruction campaign was launched.

Through the efforts of King Jan Sobieski, the interior of Warsaw's Royal Castle was refurbished in a mature Baroque style. Sobieski's suburban palatial residence in Wilanów was also built in the Baroque style. It was envisaged as a monument to the monarch's glory and splendour. Wilanów Palace combined elements of the Old Polish gentry manorhouse, the Italian Baroque villa and the French conception entre cour et jardin. It was designed and erected from 1677 to 1696 by Sobieski's court architect and secretary, Augustyn Locci.

As a votive offering to thank God for Poland's victory over the Turks in Vienna in 1683, King Jan Sobieski and his wife Maria Kazimiera built the Capuchin Church and the Church of the Sisters of the Holy Sacrament in Warsaw. Both were designed by the most outstanding architect of the Polish Baroque, Tylman van Gameren.

The architectural achievements of Jan III were matched by those of the Polish aristocracy. Grand Crown Marshal Herakliusz Lubomirski was the leading patron of the building arts. It was for him that Tylman van Gameren created his earliest design on Polish soil, a palace and garden complex in Puławy in the Lublin region. He took full architectural advantage of the fact that Prince Lubomirski's property was situated on a picturesque escarpment overlooking the Vistula. Tylman van Gameren also designed for Lubomirski a number of small, architecturally-kindred palatial residences

In Warsaw's extensive suburban areas of Ujazdów, Czerniaków and Mokotów, as well as the Bernardine Church in Czerniaków, which was meant to be Sobieski's mausoleum.

As part of his ambitious rivalry with the king, the voivod of Płock Jan Dobrogost Krasiński had Tyman van Gameren erect in Warsaw his most monumental and oppulent palace, which later came to be known as the Palace of the Republic.

During the reign of King Sobieski, sacral architecture together with accompanying religious paintings, arts and artistic crafts developed more prolifically than the secular. Italian artists, chiefly from the Italo-Swiss borderlands, were the builders and decorators of most of the late-Baroque churches and monasteries built in that period.

Many parish and monastic churches built in the late 17th century had drawn their artistic inspiration from the Eternal City. Foremost among them were Tylman van Gameren's St Anne's Church in Kraków and the Jesuit Church in Poznań, built according to a design by Jan Catenaci. It was marked by an expressive interior emanating all but theatrical pathos. Venetian patterns were implemented to their fullest in the Church of the Philippine Fathers in Gostyń.

The architecture of most churches built during the reign of King Jan Sobieski was marked by restraint and self-control. Their interiors were all the more a surprise with their violent late-Baroque artistry. The ornate, richly illusionistic paintings and stuccowork sought to draw the beholder into the miraculous events being depicted and incite in him a sense of religious fervour and elation.

The second half of the 17th century, in addition to the development of the Sarmatian portrait, sepulchral art and religious paintings, witnessed numerous paintings of battle-scenes, eulogising the military triumphs of King Jan Sobieski and his armies. These were used to adorn the interiors of palaces and churches.

As in the preceding century, throughout the 18th century many wooden houses of worship - Catholic, Orthodox and Protestant churches as well as synagogues - were built. The most numerous of all, however, were the newly-built wooden manorhouses of the nobility. Their basic form, resembling something of a cross between a peasant cottage and a palace, remained essentially unchanged down to the 19th century, although their decorative elements varied according the style of a given period.

Although nearly all of Poland's towns suffered serious economic regression following the wars of mid-century, the crafts, especially the artistic ones, flourished nevertheless. Their creations easily rivalled the imported works of foreign goldsmiths, artistic weavers and furniture-makers.

The interregnum that followed the death of King Jan

A view of Kraków, a woodcut from the end of 15th century.

Sobieski and the havoc caused by the Northern War (1700-1721) deepened Poland's social and economic decline, as the aristocracy consolidated their power at the expense of the state.

The reign of the Saxon kings of the Wettin Dynasty, August II the Strong and August III, lasting until 1764, led to the country's further deterioration. At the same time, there were attempts to reform the state in the spirit of the Enlightenment, and architecture, the fine arts and artistic crafts developed during that period.

Architectural and artistic activities were especially animated in Warsaw which had been devastated by unrest and the Northern War. Upon ascending the Polish throne, August II sought to emulate France's Louis XIV by implementing several bold architectural town-planning schemes. One of them was the Saxon Palace, a magnificent royal residence built to harmonise with its surroundings. Together with its parade-ground forecourt, fan-shaped garden and access streets it constituted a town-planning scheme known as the Saxon Axis.

Although many projects were created and some were implemented during the reign of August II, a large-scale building campaign did not get under way until the times of his successor, August III. It was then that the Royal Castle was rebuilt in the Franco-Saxon style, and more than 50 palace-and-garden residences were built or rebuilt in the new style in various parts of Warsaw.

The most monumental, bold and, at times, almost extravagant works of residential and religious architecture were erected beyond Warsaw along Poland's eastern borderlands. The superb palace and church architecture of the Saxon Period was enriched by the tasteful late-Baroque, Regency and Rococo sculptures and paintings that adorned those buildings' interiors and façades.

During the Saxon Period, there emerged in courtly, gentry and aristocratic circles a growing demand for portraits. A characteristic of the era was the penchant for theatrical poses and gestures as well as Baroque pomposity.

The continued development of traditional artistic crafts hinged on the affluent, oft-times sumptuous lifestyles of the courtly and aristocratic elites as well as on the liturgical needs of the Church.

Midway through the reign of August III, the first industrial establishments were set up. Wool-weaving developed in Great Poland, where craftsmen fleeing religious persecution in Silesia and Germany began arriving. At the initiative of Polish aristocrats, throughout the country workshops began springing up to meet the needs and indulge the refined tastes of the well-born.

Throughout the entire 18th century, numerous wooden churches, manorhouses and townhouses were still being built.

When King August II died in 1763, the following year Stanisław August Poniatowski was elected king, only to become Poland's last reigning monarch. The first years of his reign were devoted to military and treasury reforms, after which he set about implementing a broadly-sketched cultural and educational programme.

Warsaw, which was now evolving into a modern capital, was the centre of political, economic and artistic life. At the king's initiative, a town-planning scheme was launched in Ujazdów. What was known as the Stanislavian Axis joined Ujazdów Castle with the election field in Wola.

The monarch concentrated his main architectural and decorative efforts on rebuilding and modernising the Royal Castle. He also established his summer residence on the site of the former animal park at the foot of Ujazdów in what is now known as Łazienki Park. Paintings played an important role in decorating both royal residences. The position of chief royal architect was entrusted to Dominik Merlini. Marcello Bacciarelli served as chief painter, decorator and manager of the royal atelier, and Jakub Monaldi and Andrzej Lebrun were the court sculptors. At his court, the king gathered other artists as well as writers who together constituted something of a Royal Cultural Council.

An important royal initiative was the founding of the Knights' School in Warsaw in 1765. Eight years later, the king established the Commission of National Education,

Europe's first secular education ministry.

When King Stanisław August was developing his Łazienki summer residence and park, members of his family and aristocratic houses aligned with the royal court were busy creating their own residences. Usually they reflected the romantic influence emanating from England and France.

In Warsaw and environs as well as in other part of Poland the building of many neo-classical palaces and manorhouses of varying size got under way. Featuring colonnaded porticoes, they were closely tied to Poland's architectural tradition and the Polish landscape.

As a result of Warsaw's exceptional socio-economic position during the reign of Stanisław August Poniatowski, in addition to the royal court, gentry and aristocracy, an increasing role in its development was played by the well-to-do burgher class. In various parts of the capital they built townhouses which often performed commercial functions or served as hotels. The more affluent burghers, notably bankers, emulated the Polish aristocracy by building residential villas far from the institutions in which they worked.

In general, the rationalistic Age of Enlightenment was not conducive to church-building. Nevertheless, thanks to initiatives by the king, the aristocracy and affluent burghers, in this area too much was accomplished both in central Poland and Great Poland as well as in the country's eastern marches.

Through the financial efforts of Warsaw's wealthy burghers and with the personal approval of the king, a monumental Lutheran Church was erected according to the design of Szymon Bogumił Zug. Based on the severe prototype of the Pantheon in Rome, this was the most magnificent example of neo-classicist church architecture of the Stanislavian period. Wawrzyniec Gucewcz also drew inspiration from ancient temples when be rebuilt Wilno's formerly Gothic cathedral in the neo-classical style. Portrait art, which was extensively cultivated in royal circles, became widely imitated among members of the aristocracy and gentry. Parallel to the still encountered conservative Sarmatian portrait, ever more frequently portraits that broke with that tradition began appearing. That was largely the work of two popular court artists: Jan Chrzciciel Lampi and Józef Grassi. In addition to them and their compatriot Marcello Bacciarelli, the demand for portraits in Poland was also met by talented native artists led by Aleksander Kucharski and Franciszek Smuglewicz.

An important role in the art of the Stanislavian Period was played by artistic crafts. In addition to the import of numerous decorative items from England and France meant to adorn the interiors of aristocratic palaces and villas, the demands of the art and crafts market were also met by native Polish artisans.

The culmination of the more than three-decade-long reign of Stanisław August was the "Government Law" adopted by the Great Sejm (parliament) on 3 May 1791. It was Europe's first democratic constitution, and second in the world only to the US Constitution of 1787.

Government based on the new principles of a constitutional monarchy created a chance to extricate the state from its political crisis. The Poles, however, was unable to avail themselves of that opportunity, because Russia launched the third partition of Poland and was joined therein by Prussia and then Austria. In 1795, after the Russians had ruthlessly crushed the Kościuszko Insurrection that had erupted in defence of the constitution, what was left of Poland was carved up by the three aggressive powers. Tsarina Catherine forced Stanisław August Poniatowski to abdicate and Poland ceased to exist as an independent state.

The partitions produced tragic consequences for Poland. It meant not only a 120-year-long period of enslavement, not only economic exploitation and extermination, painful burdens and national persecution. The partitions also meant that the country's renewal and development begun during the Stanislavian Period had come to an abrupt halt. But although the political unity of Polish lands

Warsaw. Royal Castle in 1939.

had been shattered, the bonds between individual parts of the homeland were not destroyed They were linked together by a common struggle for independence, a national culture, a common language, a literature written in the native tongue, as well as Polish music, paintings and graphic arts.

But the echo of the partitions had scarcely subsided, when Polish Legions, commanded by General Jan Henryk Dąbrowski, were formed in Italy in 1797 at the side of France and her allies. The Legions' hymn "Poland has not yet perished" ("Jeszcze Polska nie zgnięła") in time became the Polish national anthem.

As a result of the Napoleonic Wars, a Duchy of Warsaw was established in 1807 with its capital in Warsaw. After the fall of Napoleon, the Congress of Vienna in 1815 set up on a portion of Poland's former territory a Kingdom of Poland, an entity linked by personal union to Imperial Russia.

Evidence that the enlightened ideals of the Stanislavian Period were being continued was provided when the

Warsaw Society of Friends of Learning was set up in 1800. It was Poland's first academy of arts and sciences. Seven years later, a Chamber of Education was established to deal with problems of education and training. In order to develop Polish culture and instil a respect in Polish society for national traditions, in 1800 Princess Izabela Czartoryska established in Puławy the first Polish museum. The then owner of Wilanów, Stanisław Kostka Potocki, in 1805 opened to the public the former palace of King Jan Sobieski with all its extensive collections of art and historical mementoes.

Neo-classicism had been the architectural and artistic heritage of the Stanislavian Period. In the Duchy of Warsaw and Kingdom of Poland periods it was continued mainly by Poles. They included the architects Stanisław Zawadzki and Jakub Kubicki, the sculptors Paweł Maliński and Jakub Tatarkiewicz and the painters Kazimierz Wojniakowski and Aleksander Orłowski. Most of the structures going up at that time were palaces and numerous manorhouses built in all three sections of the partitioned country. De rigueur was the colonnaded portico which had so deeply taken root in the tradition of Polish national architecture.

Gentry manorhouses held an important place in that tragic period of Polish history. They became bastions of national and patriotic education, where love for the homeland and a desire to fight for its independence were enkindled.

Warsaw's development continued during the Kingdom of Poland period. It was at that time that impressive squares, presided over by magnificent public buildings, were created. Antonio Corazzi created the most impressive of them: the Great Opera Theatre and the buildings of the Revenue and Treasury Commission in Bank Square.

Industrial building got under way in the Kielce region. To the west of Warsaw the industrial towns of Zgierz and Łódź were established.

A number of neo-classical church buildings were erected in the first decades of the 19th century. They were designed by such people as Piotr Aigner in Warsaw, Międzyrzéc Podlaski and Puławy, and by Jakub Kubicki in Okuniew and Radziejowice. The somewhat stepped-up building trend of the Duchy of Warsaw and Kingdom of Poland periods provided sculptors with an opportunity to produce architectural decorations. In time, neo-classical sculpture became an art form in its own right, producing memorial monuments, religious statuary and sepulchral art.

An anti-Polish bias on the part of the tsarist government became evident in measures aimed against the liberal parliamentary opposition, the suppressing of patriotic organisations, violations of the constitution of the Kingdom of Poland and acts of violence against senior Polish officers. This led to the outbreak of an insurrection on 28 November 1830, during which the dethronement of Tsar Nicholas I as king of Poland was proclaimed. After crushing the insurrection, the Russians did away with the Kingdom of Poland as a separate entity and abolished

Polish scholarly, cultural and educational institutions. In Warsaw's beautiful residential district, Żoliborz, known for its mansions, villas and gardens, the tsarist authorities built a huge citadel in the period from 1832 to 1834 — a place where Polish patriots were imprisoned and tortured. The clearly repressive, anti-Polish policy of the tsarist authorities forced many to emigrate or to remain abroad, They included such outstanding Poles as composer Fryderyk Chopin and political leader Prince Adam Jerzy Czartoryski. The latter's Paris residence, Hôtel Lambert, became an important patriotic centre working to restore Poland's independence through the support of the Western powers.

The occupying powers meanwhile were stepping up their persecution of Poles, promoting Russification in the Russian partition zone and Germanisation in the part of Poland occupied by Prussia. The development of art was retarded, especially that which accentuated national or

Considerable popularity was also enjoyed by the Polish architects, Adam Idzikowski and Hilary Szpilowski.

The socio-economic, political and cultural situation was different in each of the three partition zones. In the Prussian partition, encompassing Great Poland, Pomerania and Silesia, the agricultural, coal.-mining and foundry industries were the best developed. In the Russian partition, it was the textile and metal-working industries that were the most expansive. In the Austrian partition, where political reprisals were the mildest, there was no pronounced economic upturn, but scholarly, cultural and artistic life developed more vigorously than in the remaining occupation zones. In Kraków, which was in the Austrian partition, the Jagiellonian University, the Academy of Arts and Sciences and the School of Fine Arts continued to function. So did Jan Kazimierz University and the Ossoliński National Institute in Lwów.

When hopes that persecution would subside under Tsar

Poznań c. 1618. A copper engraving from the work Civitate Orbis Terrarum by Braun Hogenberg.

patriotic elements. Despite the adverse conditions and the lack of state patronage, architecture continued to develop, often achieving a high level of accomplishment. In the second half of the 19th century the economy began to develop considerably, especially industry and commerce, and building also increased. The new functions of architecture gave birth to such structures as factories, market halls, banks, hotels and tenement houses. Churches, villas and palaces continued to be built as well. Extremely popular were stylised historical buildings, usually imitating mediaeval, Renaissance or even Oriental architecture.

The dynamic growth of railways in the 19th-century Kingdom of Poland necessitated the building of a big number of train stations which soon became landmarks in the country's architectural landscape.

Of the architects active at that time on Polish territory, the most prominent were the Polonised Italians, Henryk Marconi and Franciszek Maria Lanci, as well as the well-known German architect Karol Fryderyk Schinkel.

Alexander II failed to come true, in January 1863 an armed insurrection against the tsarist authorities erupted. It lasted a year-and-a-half and also engulfed Lithuania, Belarus and Volhynia (Ukraine).

The collapse of the insurrection ushered in a new wave of anti-Polish reprisals. Estates were confiscated, death penalties were handed down and people were sent to Siberia. As a result, for the time being at least, people pushed aside all thoughts of armed struggle. National issues, historical events, the struggle for independence and burning social questions were now taken up by artists and writers. The epic painter Jan Matejko, his student Jacek Malczewski and Artur Grottger spoke through the historical guises gracing their canvases. In literature there was Nobel Prize-winning novelist Henryk Sienkiewicz and Stefan Żeromski, in theatre -Stanisław Wyspiański and in opera - Stanisław Moniuszko.

Throughout the entire 19th century, the development of portrait art, landscape and scenic painting and sculpture as well as artistic crafts, increasingly backed by industry, continued without interruption. Among the hundreds of artists involved in creative activities, a special place was held by Antoni Brodowski and Henryk Rodakowski, Piotr Michałowski, Wojciech Gerson and Józef Chełmoński, Konstanty Hegel, Pius Weloński and Edward Wittig.

Thanks to the enfranchisement of the peasantry, the 19th century provided conditions for the fuller development of folk culture than previous centuries had done.

The folk-art traditions developed in the 19th century remained alive on into the 20th. But, in addition to the natural development of folk creativity, in the wooden architecture of the late 19th and early 20th centuries there emerged a tendency aimed at creating a new "national style" based on folk tradition.

Artists with links to the "Young Poland" movement, who greatly admired the new Secession style, set themselves the task of creating an independent national style based on folk tradition and art, whilst keeping step with contemporary European trends.

The centre of that movement was Kraków, at that time artistically the most active community. In the spirit of the Secession, the Society of Friends of the Fine Arts built themselves an edifice, the Old Theatre was rebuilt and the Lwów Pastry Shop of Jan Michalik was set up. The inspiration of Secession-style art made its way to all of Poland's major towns, including Warsaw, Łódź, Poznań and Lwów. The style turned up everywhere — in building, sculpture, painting, industry and artistic crafts — and became a sign of rebellion against the petty-bourgeois art of the mid-19th century and its eclecticism. A great role in shaping Secessionist art and in the development of Young Poland was played by the multi-faceted artistic activities of Stanisław Wyspiański - a playwright, poet, painter and theatre reformer.

By the close of the 19th century, European interest in the Polish cause, which had been so lively at the time of both insurrections, had faded significantly. The early 20th century brought with it certain hopes that Poland might regain her independence, since her oppressors now found themselves in opposing camps. The outbreak of the Great War between those powers in 1914 brought that hope a bit nearer. Polish military formations took up the struggle for independence on various European fronts. The biggest of them were the Polish Legions established in the Austrian partition. The commander of their First Brigade, Józef Piłsudski, later become Poland's head of state.

When the First World War ended in 1918 with the defeat of the Central Powers - Germany, Austria and Italy - Poland regained her independence, although disputes and negotiations over her final borders would continue for some time. As a result, the reborn Polish state emerged territorially much smaller than it had been before the partitions, with only a narrow access to the Baltic. Gdańsk, the main Baltic port which for centuries had been tied to Poland, received the status of a free city.

The process of creating a state organism and forming a government and parliament was interrupted in 1920 by the outbreak of the Polish-Bolshevik War and, six years later, by the May coup of Józef Piłsudski. After the Bolsheviks were defeated and the Piłsudski group came to power, the country's economic development got under way with the backing of foreign capital

Industry, building, communications and transport developed rapidly. The incomes of the urban and rural population also began to grow. Worth mentioning is the swift pace at which Poland built its new seaport of Gdynia, in view of the increasingly German domination of Gdańsk.

In the building sector, the modernistic trend, begun at the turn of the century, continued. That style had broken ties with all forms of historicism and pursued modern solutions clearly revealing a building's construction. Those tendencies were especially strong in the Warsaw community, which attached particular importance to the legibility and functionality of architecture, the conscientious implementation of designs and luxuriously-appointed interiors.

As the needs of the reborn Polish state arose, impressive edifices began emerging to house new ministries, banks, academic institutions, department stores and hospitals. The importance attached by the state and local authorities to culture was evidenced by the construction of new museum buildings: the National Museum in Warsaw and the Silesian Museum in Katowice. Valuable cultural initiatives included the establishment of the Chopin International Piano Competition in Warsaw, the Wieniawski International Violin Competition in Poznań and the National Cultural Fund.

Of great importance to arts and letters was the reactivation of universities in Warsaw and Lwów and the creation of new ones: Poznań University, the Catholic University of Lublin, the Academy of Mining in Kraków and the School of Political Studies in Warsaw.

A great success of the two decades of between-the-wars Poland was its flourishing artistic and intellectual life. On an international scale, the works of Stanisław Ignacy Witkiewicz, Bruno Schulz and Witold Ghombrowicz were precursorial in character. Władysław Reymont received the 1924 Nobel Prize for literature. Theatre, painting, sculpture and graphic arts flourished immensely.

The creation of a Central Industrial District, begun in 1936, helped to stimulate economic growth. It encompassed several dozen counties of the voivodships of Kielce. Kraków, Lublin and Lwów, where the engineering, arms and power industries were concentrated. The all-round development of Poland's economy, science. culture and education was brought to a brutal end by the outbreak of the Second World War. Poland was attacked by the powerful German war machine on 1 September 1939, and the Nazis were aided on the 17th day of the war by a Soviet invasion from the east. On the basis of a secret protocol between Berlin and Moscow, Poland was again partitioned. This was followed by the merciless extermination of the Polish and Jewish population as well as the large-scale theft and devastation of Poland's cultural properties. In spite of the occupation, the continuity of Poland's state and military authorities was maintained. They continued to

Warsaw. Panorama of the Ghetto, 1945.

function abroad in exile and created regular army units to fight alongside the Allies. There also existed an underground Polish state with its military wing, the Home Army. The Peasant Battalions, the People's Army, the Jewish Combat Organisation and other resistance groups also gave battle to the occupying forces. After the 1943 Warsaw Ghetto Uprising and the 1944 Warsaw Uprising, the Nazis turned the defiant city into a sea of rubble. Thousands of its citizens perished underneath the débris of blocks of flats and churches.

On 17 January 1945 Warsaw was liberated from Nazi occupation. The capture of Berlin on 2 May by the Soviets, aided among others by Poles, and the unconditional surrender signed by the Germans on 8 and 9 May, ended the Second World War. As a result of the big-power agreements concluded in Yalta and Potsdam, Poland received new borders and found herself in the Soviet sphere of influence.

The new statehood emerged amid sharp political struggle, extensive war damage, ubiquitous rubble and depopulation. Although a majority of Poles did not accept the new socio-political system, efforts to rebuild the country and reactivtate various fields of public life were launched. Through the gigantic efforts of Polish society, the historic Old Town districts of Warsaw, Gdańsk, Poznań and Wrocław were raised from the ruins. Nationalised palace-and-garden complexes in Łańcut, Kozłówka, Wilanów, Nieborów and Rogalin were restored, and a good share of their artworks were reclaimed from Germany. Numerous churches as well as state-administered historic monuments were restored and rebuilt. Artistic, theatrical, musical and literary life resumed. The print-runs and readership of books increased and numerous libraries were opened. Film production and radio developed, subsequently followed by television. All the pre-war academic institutions reopened. and numerous new scientific institutes began functioning. In 1951, the Polish Academy of Sciences was established, and Poland's greatest scholarly and scientific authorities sought to gain admission.

Big changes occurred in the economy which was rebuilt following extensive war damage. Many new industrial enterprises were built as well as entirely new towns such as Nowa Huta near Kraków and Nowe Tychy near Katowice. Besides industrial construction and the related prefabricated housing, new town-planning and architectural solutions emerged in towns that were being rebuilt, modernised and expanded. Initially, functional-constructivistic tendencies prevailed, but they were interrupted when the political authorities imposed the so-called socialist realism, in reality a brand of historical eclecticism. The architecture of many towns in time became dominated by a unified type of housing industrially built using big prefabricated elements.

Although the period of People's Poland did not foster good relations between the state and the Catholic Church, thanks to the unrelenting position of the Church authorities and the sacrifice of Poland's largely Catholic society, the building of new churches got under way. They varied greatly in scale as well as in terms of architectural originality and form. A visible upsurge in church-building began towards the end of the 1970s when a Pole was elected pope and took the name of John Paul II.

Although all forms of cultural endeavour were subject to severe state censorship, even under those conditions Polish artists managed to achieve success both at home as well as in the international forum. They also launched various initiatives aimed at integrating Polish culture with that of Europe and the world. The international Chopin and Wieniawski competitions were resumed. Warsaw's Musical Autumn, the International Graphic Arts Biennial in Kraków and the International Poster Biennial in Warsaw have become permanent fixtures in Poland's calendar of cultural events. In 1968, the world's first poster museum was opened in Warsaw.

he authoritarian rule of the Marxist party and the growing economic crisis of the late 1970s led to the eruption of mass strikes and social conflicts. The Independent Self-Governing Solidarity Trade Union set ups in Gdańsk engulfed the entire country and eventually brought about the collapse of the totalitarian system. As a result, a democratic state, the Third Polish Republic, emerged in 1989.

New stage in the history of the Polish state and nation had begun, involving a broad programme of reforms and integration with the European Community. In 1991, the European Cultural Centre was set up in Kraków. In 1993, the Natolin palace-and-garden complex became a branch of the College of Europe. Poland has also become actively involved in organising the annual European Heritage Days.

↑ 1. Gdańsk. Neptune's Fountain dating from the 17th-18th centuries and the town-hall with a late-gothic tower from 1454-1489. The fountain presents is at its scenic best when illuminated at night, its spray shimmering amid an array of changing, multi-coloured lights.

→ 2. Sunset on the Baltic in the vicinity of Ustka. The devastated breakwater serves as a resting place for seagulls.

← 3. The Old Town's southern panorama. St Mary's Church is seen at left and the town-hall tower -- at right.

↙ 4. The Grand Hall, also known as the Red Hall, in the Main Town-Hall, was the work of Dutch artists in the years 1591-1611. The fire-place was created by Willem van der Meer, the ceiling by Izaak van den Blocke and the allegorical pictures adorning the walls by Hans Vredeman de Vries.

↓ 5. Gdańsk's late - gothic Artus Manor was the work of Dutch architect Abraham van den Blocke who designed many other local buildings including St Mary's Church.

→ 6. The gothic 15th-century crane overlooking the River Motława in Gdańsk incorporates a wooden hoist. In recent years, many cafés and souvenir shops have been built in the vicinity for the benefit of tourists.

← 7. Adjoining Oliwa, Sopot and Gdynia on the west is an extensive area of extremely picturesque, densely-wooded hills, which constitute an additional green belt supplementing the forests that stretch along the sea. It is known as Tri-Town Scenic Park.

↑ 8. The 1188 Cistercian Abbey in Oliwa as seen in winter from Oliwa Park. Seen at right is a fragment of the Palace of the Pelpin Abbots.

↗ 9. Oliwa Cathedral, dating from the first half of the 13th century, was subsequently expanded in the latter half of that century. The central part of the façade was embellished with rococo decorations in 1771. The cathedral is the venue of concerts on the renowned organ built by Jan Wulf in 1750.

→ 10. A lane in Adam Mickiewicz Park in Oliwa, laid out in 1740-1782. The park contains an alpinarium, a palm-room and many rare species of trees.

↖ 11. The Bath House and lighthouse at the entrance to Sopot Pier. The top of the lighthouse affords a scenic view of the shoreline, beach and pier.

← 12. On frosty winter days, birds -- chiefly swans and seagulls -- flock together in secluded places between the piles supporting Sopot Pier.

↑ 13. A fragment of the fishing port at Hel. From a once-neglected coastal village, Hel has evolved into a neat and charting little town featuring numerous cafés, shops, an historic gothic church and a lighthouse.

↗ 14. A fragment of the clock-tower of Szczecin Castle with reconstructed decorations dating from 1736. Built in the 16th century, the castle has five wings and an internal courtyard.

→ 15. A landscape in the Żuławy area near Gdańsk. This depressed area abounds in tributaries of the Vistula (the Nogat, Leniwka, Szkaprawa, Motława and Święta) as well as drainage canals.

→→ 16. The gothic castle at Lidzbark Warmiński, picturesquely set on the banks of the River Łyna, was built in 1350-1400 and boasts a beautifully-arcaded internal courtyard. For 200 years the seat of Polish bishops, the castle is now a museum.

← 17. The Camedulian monastic complex and church at Wigry dates from 1704-1705. In addition to monastic buildings, the church is surrounded by the huts of hermit-monks. A monastery and huts have been turned into a holiday centre.

→ 18. Frombork Cathedral, built by the Warmia Chapter in 1329-1388, is a big, richly-appointed hall-type church. Mikołaj Kopernik (Nicolaus Copernicus) was buried in its crypts.

↓ 19. The gothic cathedral of Pelpin, which was built in the 13th, 14th and 15th centuries, ranks among Poland's biggest and most beautiful. Worth viewing in its interior are its gothic stalls and numerous other late-Renaissance, baroque and rococo appointments.

↘ 20. The church at Święta Lipka is a pilgrimage centre and architecturally ranks among the most interesting in the Masuria and Warmia regions. Its architect was Jerzy Ertly of Wilno who built it in 1687-1692. The church's late baroque polychromy from 1722-1737 was teh work of Mateusz Mayer. Perwanger of Tolkmicko designed the church's forecourt surrounded by a four-sided gallery with corner chapels adorned by 44 baroque-style sculptures. Adjoining the second pillar is a fragment of the linden-tree with a figure of the Blessed Virgin which was growing there before the church was built. Hence the name Święta Lipka (Holy Linden).

→→ 21. The Masurian Lake District is the part of Poland best known for its commercial fresh-water fisheries and angling. There are so many lakes full of fish, that the fishing is generally quite good. Shown here is a landscape of Lake Tałty.

↖ 26. The gothic castle and cathedral in Kwidzyn were built by the Teutonic Knights in the 14th century. The bridge, set on huge arched supports with a tower, was known as a 'gdanisko' or 'dansker' and served as the castle's mediaeval lavatory.

↑ 27. A well-known stud farm is situated in at Kadyny on the Vistula Lagoon along the road to Frombork.

← 28. Elbląg Canal links the towns of Ostróda and Elbląg. Owing to divergent water levels, the boats carrying tourists along this picturesque route must cross several locks and dams. At left the mechanism of one of the sluice-gates may be seen.

→ 29. The Ethnographic Park in Olsztynek contains numerous examples of wooden folk architecture brought together from throughout the Warmia and Masuria region.

↑ 30. Landscape with a windmill in Olsztyn voivodship.

← 31. Forests near Bydgoszcz.

→ 32. The Copernicus Monument in front of the gothic town-hall of Toruń, where the astronomer was born in 1473.

→ 33. The rotunda of St Prokop, built of stone blocks in Strzelno c. 1160, ranks among Poland's best-preserved romanesque churches.

↖ 34. The gothic castle at Radzyń Chełmiński was built by the Teutonic Knights in the 13th century. After Poland recovered it in 1466, it served as the seat of district authorities and courts.

←← 35. The 13th-century Bronze Doors of Gniezno, which contain 18 scenes depicting the life and martyrdom of St Wojciech, are among the most outstanding example of mediaeval artistic metal.

← 36. The huge, nearly 1,000-year-old oaks in the park of Rogalin Palace are the biggest concentration of old oaks in Europe. Some of them have a circumference of 9 metres.

↑ 37. Construction of this rococo-classicist palace in Rogalin was begun c. 1770 and was completed in the early 19th century by the outstanding Warsaw architects Dominik Merlini and Jan Christian Kamsetzer.

→ 38. The Renaissance castle in Gołuchów, dating from c. 1560, was rebuilt in the latter half of the 19th century in the style of the French Renaissance. Up until 1939 it was the private museum of the aristocratic House of Czartoryski, but during the Second World War its collection was carted off to Germany. A portion of its objets d'arts was recovered after the war. At present it is a branch of the National Museum of Poznań.

→→ 39. A scenic view of the Great Poland National Park in the vicinity of Lake Dymaczewskie.

↖ ↖ 40. The Poznań town-hall, rebuilt in 1550-155 following a fire by Jan Baptysta Quadro in the style of the North Italian Renaissance, features a beautiful façade with semi-circular arcades and an open loggia.

↖ 41. The Renaissance-style Hall of Rebirth in the Poznań town-hall, also known as the Grand Hallway, dates from 1555 and was the most elegant interior of its kind in Eastern Europe. The Grand Hallway's coffer-type vaulting, supported by external pillars, was the work of Jan Baptysta Quadro in 1550-1560. The town-hall has a classicist tower built in 1781-1783 by Jan Christian Kamsetzer.

← 42. The Golden Chapel in Poznań Cathedral was the work of Franciszek Maria Lanci. It serves as the mausoleum of Prince Mieszko I and King Bolesław the Brave. It was built in 1815-1840 in the Byzantine style which at that time was regarded as the style of the first Piast rulers. The most beautiful part of the entire cathedral, the chapel is full of gilded decorations and rich ornamentation and has a mosaic floor. Above the sarcophagus are the sculpted figures of Mieszko I and Bolesław the Brave.

↑ 43. Kórnik Castle, dating from the early 16th century, was rebuilt in the first half of the 19th century in the English gothic style. It now houses the Kórnik Library whose collection exceeds 150,000 tomes, including the manuscripts of the romantic poets Mickiewicz and Słowacki.

→ 44. The faithful don their regional folk costumes to take part in processions on the feast of Corpus Christi in Złaków Kościelny near the town of Łowicz.

← 45. The baroque palace in Nieborów was built in 1690-1696 according to a design by Tyman of Gameren. It was last owned by the aristocratic House of Radziwiłł. Its richly-appointed interiors now house a branch of the National Museum of Warsaw. Next to it stands a majolica workshop with a tradition of many centuries.

↙ 46. The Red Salon, the most beautiful interior of Nieborów Palace, contains a well-known portrait of Anna Orzelska, daughter of King August II and Henryka Duval (painted in the salon of Antoine Pesne c. 1735).

→ 47. The fortified church in Brochów, built in 1554-1561, was where the baptism of Fryderyk Chopin took place. It was partially reconstructed following the damage it sustained in the First World War.

↓ 48. This manorhouse at Żelazowa Wola was the birthplace of Fryderyk Chopin (22 February 1810). It contains a museum of mementoes left behind by the great Polish pianist and composer. Concerts of Chopin's music are held there in summer.

→→ 49. Warsaw's Old Town Marketplace. During the summer season numerous cafés remain open until late at night for the benefit of tourists seeking refreshment.

←← 50. The statue of the Little Insurrectionist near the defensive walls of Warsaw's Old Town commemorates the children who fought in the 1944 Warsaw Uprising.

← 51. Wilanów Palace, was built in the style of the Italian baroque by Augustyn Locci. in the latter half of the 17th century. Surrounded by a beautiful formal gardens and an expansive park, it was the summer residence of King Jan III Sobieski.

↙ ↙ 52. Warsaw's 43-storey Palace of Culture and Science was built in the period of socialist realism (1952-1955). It contains numerous exhibition halls, cinemas, theatres and museums as well as a 3,000-seat Congress Hall.

↙ 53. Banks and many other Polish and foreign institutions have their offices in the "Blue Skyscraper" in Warsaw's Bankowy Square.

↗ 54. Warsaw's Royal Castle with the King Zygmunt III Column. The former gothic castle of the Masovian Princes was rebuilt and expanded for King Zygmunt August in 1596-1972 by Franciszek Parr and Jan Baptysta Quadro. From 1596 to 1794 it was the official residence of Poland's kings and the place where parliament proclaimed the Constitution of the Third of May in 1791.

→ 55. The Palace in Warsaw's Łazienki Park was the private residence of King Stanisław August Poniatowski. Originally the bathhouse of the Lubomirskis, it was rebuilt in the latter half of the 17th century by Tylman of Gameren. The park surrounding the palace ranks among the most beautiful of its kind in Europe.

→→ 56. The Fryderyk Chopin Monument in Łazienki Park was designed by W. Szymanowski in 1926. Destroyed in the last war, it has since been restored. In summer, Chopin piano recitals are held at its base.

57. The fruit-growing industry has developed intensively in the Grójec area. This is where Warsaw gets most of its fruit from.

58. The baroque interior of the Shrine of the Black Madonna on Bright Mountain in Częstochowa. Adjoining the church is the chapel containing the miraculous icon of Our Lady of Częstochowa, the legendary Black Madonna, which attracts many-thousand-strong pilgrimages from across Poland and abroad.

59. The church and monastery complex on Bright Mountain in Częstochowa gained renown for withstanding the Swedish siege of 1655. Built in 1382, it was subsequently expanded and rebuilt in the years that followed. Its tower soars to a height of 105 metres.

60. On a tall hill in the Kraków-Częstochowa Jura stand the ruins of the once mighty Ogrodzieniec Castle dating from the 13th and 14th centuries. Rebuilt in 1530-1543 by S. Boner, it was burnt down by the Swedes in 1655.

← 61. The Sandomierz town-hall is seen emerging from the morning mist. Built in the 16th century, it features a beautiful Renaissance attic.

↙ 62. The Bernardine Church at Leżajsk dating from 1618-1628 and contains what is undoubtedly one of the most magnificent organ in Poland. Built in the later half of the 17th century, it was expanded in 1716.

↓ 63. A fragment of the mannerist Renaissance townhouses belonging to Mikołaj and Krzysztof Przybył in the marketplace of Kazimierz Dolny. Built in 1615, their rich decorative stonework continues to command admiration and reflects the mannerist tendency to fill all empty spaces.

→ 64. Zamoyski Palace at Kozłówka was originally built in the baroque style in 1740 but was rebuilt towards the end of the 19th century. At present it is a Museum of Palatial Interiors. One of its wings houses Poland's only museum of socialist realism.

↘ 65. Łańcut Castle, built in 1624-1641, was rebuilt following a 1688 fire with the assistance of Tyman of Gameren. In the late 18th and early 19th century, it was thoroughly rebuilt by its then owner, Izabela née Czartoryska Lubomirska. To carry out that project she engaged some of the most outstanding artists of the period including Bogumił Zug and Christian Kamsetzer.

← 66. The town-hall in the town of Zamość, known as the 'pearl of the Polish Renaissance', was built in 1639-1651 and partially rebuilt in 1591-1600 by Bernardo Morando.

↑ 67. The 1750 wooden Eastern Orthodox church from Rosolin in the Bieszczady Mountains may now be admired in the Sanok Ethnographic Park.

↗ 68. This Eastern Orthodox church built at Kwiatoń in 1700 is one of the most interesting to be found anywhere in the High Beskid, Low Beskid and Bieszczady Mountains.

→ 69. This 1805 Eastern Orthodox church at Komańcza is one of many found in the Bieszczady Mountains.

→→ 70. A panorama of the Bieszczady Mountains with a view of the Połonina Caryńska mountain pasture. These picturesque hills with their mild slopes are a great attraction to devotees of long hikes.

← 76. The Confession of St Stanisław, created by Giovanni Trevano in 1620-1629, stands at the centre of Wawel Cathedral. The relics of St Stanisław are kept in a special silver coffin.

→ 77. Prądnik Valley with the 18-metre-tall rock formation Hercules' Club and the 14th-century Castle on Pieskowa Skała. One of Poland's most beautiful knights' castles, it features an arcaded courtyard. It now contains a museum.

↓ 78. At Tyniec near Kraków, on a tall stone cliff overlooking the Vistula stands a Benedictine Abbey. Its original romanesque features were rebuilt and a monastery garden was added in the 17th century.

← 79. Morskie Oko (Eye of the Sea) is the biggest and most beautiful lake in the Tatra Mountains. A mountain hostel overlooks the lake which covers an area of 34.5 hectares and plunges to a depth of 51 metres.

↓ 80. A view of Mount Giewont (1,894 above sea-level) from the vicinity of Zakopane.

→ 81. A view of the Tatra Mountains and Mount Giewont at sunset, when dramatic scenery is created by the silhouetted mountain contours, trees and red-glowing sky.

← 82. Along the road between Kuźnice and Kalkatówki, next to the Church of the Albertine Sisters is the hermit's hut of Blessed Brother Albert (1846-1918), the founder of the mendicant Albertine Order.

↑ 83. Three Crowns (982 metres above sea-level) is the tallest peak in the Pieniny Mountains. The mountain slopes are full of jagged rock formations covered by dense mixed forests, and their flora numbers 100 different species.

→ 84. The Renaissance castle of the Piast Princes in Brzeg on the Odra was built in 1544-1560 round existing gothic walls. It was erected round a four-sided courtyard as a three-winged residential building with a curtain wall on the west. In that period the castle was fitted with three-storey Renaissance-style galleries. They were the work of Italian architects Józef and Jakub Parr. The galleried courtyard was patterned on Wawel Royal Castle. The gate-house is adorned with the beautifully-sculpted busts of the Piasts.

← 85. The tombs of the Silesian Piasts in St Ann's Chapel (1309) in Opole's Franciscan Church, built in the latter half of the 14th century.

↓ 86. Daisy von Pless' study, one of the interiors of the huge 12th-century Pszczyna Castle which was rebuilt in 1873. It belonged to the princely House of Hochberg von Pless, one of Germany's wealthiest aristocratic families. At present it contains a Museum of Castle Interiors.

→ 87. Wrocław's gothic town-hall was built of brick and stone in the latter half of the 13th century. Its rich exterior décor was added in 1471-1504. It features a 66-metre-tall tower with a ceramic peak. Its most valuable features are the sculptures and eastern portal dating from 1328. The building is now a museum. .

→→ 88. Wrocław Central Station is one of Poland's most interesting railway stations. It features highly diversified architecture and extensive facilties -- shops, cafés, service facilities, etc. Despite the station's huge dimensions, all its platforms are found beneath a glass roof. .

← 89. This beautiful, historic building situated along a River Odra canal is the Ossolineum containing and contains a valuable collection of manuscripts and old prints brought from Lwów. The building was erected in 1734-1755.

↙ 90. Wrocław's Cathedral of St John the Baptist was built in stages, beginning in 1244, and its hull and tower were completed in the 14th century. Although 70% of its interior was destroyed in the last war, many valuable objects managed to survive.

↓ 91. The capacious building of Wrocław University, which measures 200 metres in length, was built in 1728-1742 and ranks among Central Europe's most splendid baroque edifices. Aula Leopoldina is a magnificent interior, replete with impressive sculptures and polychromy. The frescoes were executed by Krzyzstof Handke of Olomouc and the polychromy -- by Franciszek Józef Mangold.

← 92. This Mausoleum of the Silesian Piasts is found in Lubiąż Cathedral which is part of an 18th-century Cistercian Abbey. It is a huge, three-nave basilica with a rich baroque interior.

↙ 93. The 13th-century little Norwegian timber Church of Wang was purchased and moved to this spot by Prussian King Friedrich Wilhelm IV in 1841. Its most valuable elements are original fragments containing Viking motifs.

↓ 94. Wilczka Falls at Międzygórze plunge into a gneissic ravine in the midst of a dense forest. Międzygórze is the starting point for those entering the Śnieżnik Massif (elevation 1,425 metres), the highest point in the Kłodzko area and the Eastern Sudeten Mountains.

←← 95. More than 100 fantastically-shaped rock formations developed in the Karkonosze Mountains during the Ice Age. Shown here is one known as the Pilgrims, situated along a tourist trail leading to Mount Śnieżka.

→ 96. Mount Śnieżka (1,602 metres), the highest peak in the Karkonosze Range, seen in winter. Poland's border with the Czech Republic runs along the peak.

↓ 97. An upstream stretch of the Szklarka, one of the many streams in the Szklarska Poręba area, is seen before a waterfall by the same name. The streams flow through a forest replete with rock formations known as monadnocks.